Alan John Stubbs was born in Salford and now lives and works in Cumbria. He is a prize winner in the Arvon International Poetry Competition 2008, was a finalist in the Mirehouse Poetry Prize 2007, and has been shortlisted for the Bridport Prize. This is his first poetry collection and first collaborartion with The Onslaught Press. Several poems not included in this collection can be found in the Onslaught anthology *to kingdom come: voices against political violence* (2016) edited by Rethabile Masilo.

Fiona Sampson has been shortlisted twice for the T.S. Eliot and Forward Prizes. Her work has been translated into more than thirty languages, and awarded a Cholmondeley Award, the Newdigate Prize and the Ziaten Prsten (Macedonia) among others. A Fellow and Council Member of the Royal Society of Literature, she is Professor of Poetry at the University of Roehampton and is the Editor of *Poem* magazine.

other poetry titles from The Onslaught Press

We Want Everything (2016) Moe Seager
to kingdom come (2016) edited by Rethabile Masilo
Behind the yew hedge (2015) Gabriel Rosenstock & M. Staunton
Antlererd Stag of Dawn (2015) Gabriel Rosenstock
Bumper Cars (2015) Athol Williams
Waslap (2015) Rethabile Masilo
Aistear Anama (2014) Tadhg O Caoinleain
for the children of Gaza (2014) M. Staunton & R. Masilo (eds.)
Poison Trees (2014) Philippe Saltel & Mathew Staunton

The Lost Box of Eyes

Alan John Stubbs

The Onslaught Press

Published in Oxford by **The Onslaught Press**
11 Ridley Road, OX4 2QJ
March 2016

ISBN-13: **978-0-9934217-3-0**

Typeset in Le Monde Livre & Le Monde Sans,
designed, & edited by **Mathew Staunton**
Printed by Lightning Source

Acknowledgements & Thanks

I thank the following for their understanding and help:
Fiona Sampson, Marion McCready, Terry Jones, Graham Williams,
Tony Brown, John Metcalfe, Jon Tait, Mathew Staunton,
and all of my friends;

the following magazines for publishing some of the poems in this book;
*Agenda, Dreamcatcher Poetry Monthly, Poetry Review, The Rialto,
Carillon, The Cannon's Mouth*;

my family: Kathleen, Emma, Rachel, Rebecca,
Ava and Dylan, Dad (Alan Trevor), Mum (Mavis),
my brothers Andrew and David, and all of their families,
and Matthew and Laurence.

To Kathy with love

Preface

Huddled under the lid

Compounds and Fire

In the corner where sleep gathers

Preface

Alan Stubbs writes like no-one else. That's a hugely important thing to say about a poet. Yet for the poet himself, it can feel like a mixed blessing to be "out there", "on a limb", at the waney edge of practice itself; for all the world like this book's exiled 'Ovid at the water'. Another way to say this is that a poet like Stubbs has to have enormous artistic courage. To the quotidian terror of the blank page, he must add the vertiginous realization that every new poem requires from him nothing less than a complete reinvention of poetic form.

This is not to suggest that Stubbs's darkly narrative book is a Macedonian salad of styles and projects. On the contrary: a deep coherence underlies the work. Images and register recur and, in recurring, speak at angles to themselves. A consistently angry, inelegant and anti-elegant imaginary is at work here, with equal detail, on both the inhabited local world and dystopian fantasy, relationship and place, language and image.

Stubbs's ever-expanding verse often has a motor of narrative, but it is also impelled by urgent tone and by frequently risky thought-experiment. There is curiosity, too, and an energetically appropriative take on the world, particularly the world this book's "narrator" travels to. 'Ithaca' may be imagined or real, but Florence, in 'in Firenze art', is embodied in the marble of Michelangelo's David, while a Turkish coastline from Nazim Hikmet's work is reconstructed in 'On the days'. *The Lost Box of Eyes* takes us to New York, Havana, Prague and Madrid, and its cosmopolitan sophistication is a useful rejoinder to the reader who assumes that the passionate concentration with which other poems detail English birds and trees is a sign of a local imagination: of some latter-day John Clare, single-handedly modernizing English verse.

It is no such sign. Yet Stubbs is like Clare in the stubborn courage of his unique poetics; and in its rootedness in a vividly re-rendered materiality. These "nature" poems are hyper-real; as absolutely contemporary as any urban anecdote. And these thought experiments repeat no single theory, but place everything comfortable and comforting from musical formal tropes to the so-readily-digested argumentation of lyric conventions in question.

When I first came across Alan Stubbs's work, among the submissions to a magazine, I was reading tens of thousands of unsolicited poems a year. I was punch-drunk with the repeated strategies and repetitive ideas that dominated and still dominate if not British verse as a whole, then the whole middle ground of that verse. I was, as any committed reader of verse must be, frequently bored by the riskless, irreproachable poetry I so often found arranged on the page before me. Alan Stubbs's poetry, by contrast, came searing off the page: restless, energetic, uncomfortable and discomforting, like a call to poetic arms. And so it does today.

Fiona Sampson
Coleshill, 12th February, 2016

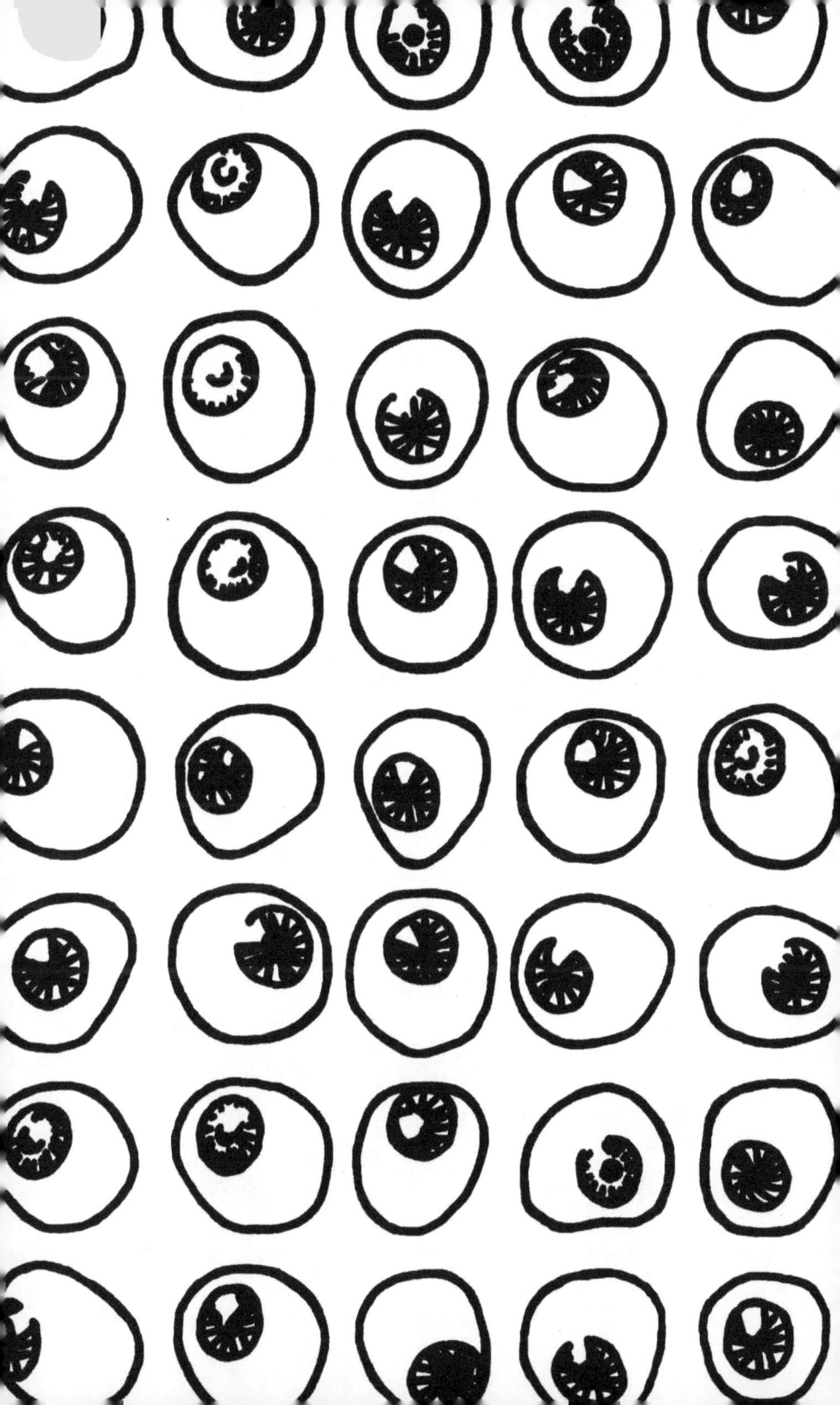

Huddled under the lid

a philosophical provocation

this tree is both an assertion and a dialogue
it is ambiguous and playfully sets out in branches
it is rooting too slowly to appreciate in inches
it is not just itself but also lichens and mosses
aggregate on its surfaces, and the spine of trunk
is a book of record in a way, and the flat leaf
a translator of light and air and water, a sheathe
of cares where a slaughter of aphids turn gunk
and tear into a million chews, or that tree frogs
may choose to hide beneath and snooze, or foxes
paw at when they parachute loose, and so this
is an interpretation, and that is all it is, a miss
heard call, a faint echo, an accumulation of
words sighing like leaves on a tree, or a stove
that is ready to cook the meal that's inside it.
This door is blind shut and we don't know it's lit.

Leaf Cutters

I was thinking of the leaf cutters
as if they were Indian tradesmen sitting cross legged
at a low bench fretting
with a fine toothed saw

wood, a thin dust, coloured the floor
as pale as the butter
she would paddle to a block and set aside

I was thinking of the blind lives
waiting on the fat of the land
—how a smoulder of sun could turn
to a rich slobber

the pond would be a thick soup in summer
everything pressed close in together

the worn out shapes lost in the heat

The beginning

her eyelids are leaves
rain softens
kohl black about the rims

the fire behind them releases all of the hot trapped energies of plants
the chaos of trees

suns would close up or disappear
we would fall through the holes we found in stones
frogs would swell up in our throats
butterflies fly about our stomachs
and the needles in our arms and legs would turn towards the north
where the ice cities of the winds are
desolate and trees grow thorns they spit that impale us
sooner or later
fixing us one to the other so that the raw clay might be pushed one
into the other making
the idea of the thing

Mouth

a piece of work it speaks of propulsion
on wings of thin
tissue fixed on wires sprung of a hunch back
bunch of muscles firing
feeling up from the surface to the air

a blink of feathers
fine filament settles to pierce and draw
plasma unfelt
mouths needle becoming a part
the heart
pumps momentarily to

the succour it savours
a heat that lifts
however briefly

A body of ice is hot

Such a continent of white
      hands painted onto bared shoulders
            palms out-spread-fingered form angels wings
                  a place no person has been
Or could ever have been
      when it's thirteen million eight hundred square kilometres
of ice
      water, held,
          solid celled in matrices of atoms

If you open your mouth and make a hollow
          of your cheeks
             head swaddled in black linen
             you can blow
      out the wind flickered candle flame
and move lines of light
      And as time passes
          lines like ropes are tricked into a face
          onto skin
And sound washes over all, taut
        streaming as the smoke is blown

Touch the warm tight surface, rib bones lift, shoulders arch
        and in the darkness, colour
          two people sitting at table
           under a low light
             drinking coffee

Reds rust, blue is electric blue, and there is an intensity of cold
        but yellows and browns illuminate this undarkness
          and shapes play
        play into themselves, into each other
               exploring

Sheets billow and a solo piano
           wire taut sound-hums-as notes decay
                      making an end of themselves

And outside clouds are icebergs floating, tip visible
         in their white-blue-sky-country above the living greens

while here in this vacuum two nipples swell to rosebuds
        and the cottages bare plaster walls become skin
                to the two bodies that lie soaking within
                      one soft cunt
                        luxuriously
                          warm and wet
Taking as much time
         cock swollen rigid
           as they can to bathe in the glowing orange light
outside of the striplight honesty
           They are
Outside of the crowds
        arms raised, bodies swaying
           that rise from under music
              to become apparent over music
                  or be within it, ears popping
                  high on atmosphere

And a sleeping bag is needed to maintain the bodies temperature,
                        its heat
                      even here

Out there sunlight warms skin
        and in such confusing surroundings it is impossible

to know just where you are
                and where you end
                      and you can lose yourself
eyes closed gripping the bottom lip tight between your teeth

Should you taste blood, relax
          warm red iron rich blood
                    can rest to a hard clot
even though trees may guard it
and water is released, freed, flows like the melting of a thick ice
          sheet
                    of the blue-white-Antarctic
                      pulsing into sea

When eyes shut
          anonymous people blend into one amorphous body
                cells, each with no purpose
                    except to be there at this time
                    and move together

And what is always absent is everything else

As they dance

Roughly crashing about the chairs and tables
pushed out to the edges of the floor,
eyes fix on each other
and are withdrawing themselves even as they reveal
some part of what it is that they want,
or would rather be.

If I took a black and white
the interest would be in the shading where
one definite thing slowly becomes another.
The smudging of boundaries always there
that appears, however fleetingly,
clear to the eye

when worse for wear.
So that when the man places two hands on the woman's breasts
admiringly, and they are allowed to rest
like plates snugged warm
as if they are a claim
a protection of the full nest
in the storm to come,

fulfilling a purpose that only now came upon them
it is the motion of the planets made it happen.

Haaf

Spoke about the haaf
nets common on the estuary
when a catch was more important;
sands sucked our shoes petulantly,
gulls wading rose, or embedded about us,
with everything moved towards the gaping mouth
aware of the gripped drift outwards,
the seas taking.

We stepped testingly delicate,
shifting our weight,
balance and mass measured across a surface
that might not take us,
so that almost a mishear, almost there,
we are out where the deep is

Love can be a spike

A smartly dressed man attends a young boy
with lank brown hair, spooning for him
as he eats his soup, and using a napkin
to wipe away the escapes of his flaccid lips.
He fixes his headband, the type
an athlete might wear, more firmly.

Each end of the headband is attached
to the boys chair, so that when it moves
his head will be held securely in place
and not nod forwards, uncomfortably,
on the thin stalk his neck is. But take

every strain. The elegant man smiles
roughs the boys hair, spiking it fashionably,
tenderly, with affection.
                              Spikes
like those that project from a conker shell
that grow to protect, to absorb a fall,
deflecting hurt from the delicate
nut cradled safe in its thick green womb
so that it might ripen, and grow soon.

The man tidies the lunch things onto trays.
Pushes the chairs back under the table.
Then, as he wheels the boy away
his fingers say again what he couldn't say.

Ivy

Hard days striking pyramid flowers from the way
breaking towering green stalks poked vainly past leafy stems
uprooting a strangling morass that cut back reveals
colonies of snails clustered tight, hid safe, and spiders
scurrying from branch to brick tenderly skeletal
their webs fluttering flags of grey that catch the bright sunlight
of a dying summers day—light falling only to rise again
warmed and mocking those holding to a hardened past
fastened by the millipede tendrils that line the cracked patina
of old wall to run, hanging, in the air, brushing hands
with a fine dust of age so rich it clogs the lungs and slows the veins
to an old pulse that begs a change, a change

swollen blood berries sign another growth each clot shiny
and exposed, its stems hooked sharp with hungry thorns to
graze and pierce, protecting them from soft skin

loose bricks fixed in place after a stand of a hundred years
are bones to an invader that climbed, covered, crumbled,
and clothed them in green and black, brought in other refugees
from the blocked light, and then cascaded to ground
to force victory with a stamp of its twisted, gnarled, foot

now a cautious shuffler unused to its ploughed furrow feels
with chisel and saw to prise and pull apart, peeling stems to cut
so that keener feet can rise in place of the long dead and reverse
a deathly tread—an early release of blood saps strength
with clouded thoughts of work and bed, but the ivy holds
while others with a mornin' smile or nod pass by on the pavement's
tacky rings of autumn that drop from high leaves like shadows
to hold them for an instant from the light, aware of broken apples

bruised brown that invite younger feet, or bright suddenly call butterflies
to erratic flight against the stiff breeze starting branches to motion
whipping up the leaves, directing eyes to chase winged eyes
past the bird lovers who gather on this day each month, religiously,
flocking to share caged passions, their feathered triumphs
carried before them in the last of the good light

lost to this in a pollen haze of work, while each detail points
and plays in the sun that catches easy strollers
rolling slowly through their days, the cutting carries on
to a nothing where things come—

Growth

Late watering half a kettle full the tangling cheeseplant
I see the strange round green roots that it shoots all angles
blindly seeking more, feeling in amongst electric cables
that feed computers, printers, heaters, from a whole
bunch of sockets on the floor.
                              If this room was
organic there would have evolved a purpose in all of this
mesh.
Like the greening spread that reaches beyond
I would not have it any other way.

there are four boats and her

they are hollowed out and gaily painted half eggshells all
too delicate in their ribbings to be let to sea in the skirmishing
winds, and have been pulled up onto sandy ridges
to rest a safe distance from the sucking lips at the waters edge.

they are allowed the journeys of small children
perhaps slipping out to as far as the new marina where
the shiny metallic cabin cruisers are, and back,
and they can be abandoned here safely without a
thought that they might be taken away, swallowed up, or disappear.

the beach is the colour of peach flesh muted by a thin dust
layer, and the sea is a blue felt flecked with grey. She

faces out to sea, and
is a broad curvy pole that the flags of black taffeta skirt and dark hair
are anchored to. She

is the only person in view. Her
shadow, and each row-boat, roots the shifting grains
of the soft beach that ripple in waves. There is

something unreal about the boats, as if they are models,
sketches for the real thing, or insubstantial in some way, but she

is darker than her shadow, and is
strong shoulders, torso, hips and legs all alert to changes
happening
in the waves, and in the skies shifting and blowing
that trick the seas up into plays
of whites, and darken with threats of grey

watery depths, and she stands resisting all the spits
and pellets wind raises, shields her face, and looks
out towards what is coming in
behind the clouds, and waits

note d'hôtel

On the reverse of a *note*
for a Paris hotel—August 2000
I write this
backwards almost
instead of engaging in conversation
just now, for which two mouths and two ears,
are needed. To be correct
we filled that double room, or *chambre*
with just the right number of days
on that occasion. Four nights

from the fourteenth to the seventeenth.
What happened?
Was it so hot then, that hot
glistening summer?
And I remember, or sense still, the smell of her
her taste
slaking.
And the small intimate lift
that took us both there
touching all the way up, so close together.

And reading the invoice now I'm surprised to see
One hundred francs for two *petits-déjeuners*.

the first to pass was

a Dog, almost a Wolf, but packed.
A Husky in a rig of leather straps

tight–tethered to the steering column
handle-bars made into bull horns

—of the bicycle he sat on
steering the long corners

of the park by the river.
He was a blur.

He'd worked away all year
in the Green Zone—in Iraq

after the work at home dried up
doing recon-

struction for big money
through an agency. He

said they paid because they did not trust
the locals to make good. And that

everything there came down the road
from around here—the soldiers gear—the

whole of the breaking apart, and re-con
-structing. The muscular

dog was dirty silver running
hard, all shoulders, and the massive head

salivating open—aired a blood
tongue that lolled on saw teeth, as if

it rested on a feather bed. Its
skeleton sides heaved with the effort

of it—of all the pulling
after something that is nothing

Broad Street

the old spiral carpet encircled us there
in the bay window sheltering from rain.
eating chips, poor chips, the smell of fat pervading
the room, as we used up time before leaving
for the train. We clustered awhile imagining what?
certainly not the coming reality of the years
centred on children, young voices, faces, all that care,
but deciding whether or not to move in and occupy
such a property, this long empty cavernous house
so grand after the close council built home

we were leaving. In the end the difference was the trees.
their closeness, the stature of them in single file flanking
the road, a ribbon of wildness breaking into it unevenly by root,
and flagging the season in green, and calling shadow
to chase the suns move through each day, a vague finger
tracing times path over cobbles and pavements, sometime even
to this white door. Or maybe it was the glory of coloured glass
in the hallway; an artisan work flooded by lights streaming
through the summer applying red and blue to walls
or floor, warming their cold skin, that sealed it.

In the pause that followed
our children ran the length of each room, tried all the taps
used the toilet, opened every closet door, accustomed
themselves to the high ceilings, ornate plasterwork,
looked up the chimneys for evidence of fire, heat,
shouted to register the echoes beat so we couldn't be lost,
caught by the intricate weave of this place, or be held long,
dry and alone close to the city centre; or that the high ivy walls
wouldn't fold over and enclose us, stifling our naive hopes.

Each touch of their small hands shocked life back into the brick
and the building began to breathe. In this short time
they shot through the house bringing an end to stillness,
laying every ghost, their shrill voices and clattering feet
rebounding in the hall, possessing every brick and floorboard,
gathering us up and with our belongings wrapping them in years,
delivering them here to be with their imprint, and ours. turning all

that which is, was

dad lit the coals
bought together on old newspapers and kindling in the grate
we gathered in close to
the sputter and crack of flames and soot

a glow of stories all about us
beyond the glare cold had dominion—we huddled
small in the armchairs embrace

a thumb mouse rattled from the fires brass
surround and was lost to
the enclosing blackness

we remained
thinking of the wild

memory a small fire . . .

Madrid

is the Man running for a bus
blood pounding, sounding
through the Man running for a bus up the Gran Via
the Man running for a bus up the Gran Via in a long black coat
a trailing frock coat

Is these older ladies slow-stepping off of the bus
who look down at their legs
who talk about their brown legs
sad legs, gesturing and laughing so
a petite girl with a pony-tail
                          shaped into a jug handle
                          dances up, and stops
                          just behind them
It is the two Saturns
                          Goya's Saturn
                          has the most exaggerated
                          wild staring eyes
                          and has already devoured
                          the arm of a delicate
                          son to the shoulder
                          while the Saturn of Rubens
                          is an ordinary man
                          a God with a scythe
                          time resting
                          who has only just begun
                          to tear at the pallid flesh
                          of a raised babe's chest

It is the people hanging coats
upon the high backs of chairs
the woman wearing green over-alls

who takes away all of the used
glasses and diligently wipes
the tables of spilled Mahou
Cerveza Especial that tingles
the gums, and leaves
a characteristically bitter taste

It is this, this portrait
of George Dyer sitting
before a mirror,
a portrait that has two mirrors
within it One a bisect of his paunched body
that runs from just below the left ear
that is the only ear visible
as his head turns away
to all the way down to his large black shiny lace-up shoes
His hands are undecipherable
as hands
All of the flesh is slabs of flesh
insistently
sandstone pink
the corporeal
being as unhealthy
as a sanguinely blotted blotter

The second is a plane
of reflection trapped—his turned away
face
contained on a surface
mounted onto a wooden plinth
It displays his ruddy face
as a face on a plate

fractured
in to two parts, with the deepest blue
                              of a good blue sky
                    all about it, and also within

it Madrid is

the woman in a garden with a parasol who is
just another black shape, although haloed
with a white that draws this eye in
to recognising the woman in a black dress, standing
amongst tall grasses and outlying trees and hedges sketched
a distance from the foreground that is filled
with the colours of flowers on tall stems

Except for the few instances of black
green is everywhere accompanied
by the whites and yellows and reds of the flowers
the brush strokes textures that call the movements

of air into being Madrid

is the pleasure at not understanding
this red horse that has hands where forelegs should be
and the woman who is a curve landing upon it in a curve
that mirrors the white breaking moon
who has a candle stick gripped tight
in the hands, or forelegs, that flames
and that all of these exist in the sky
of a landscape dominated by a bride and groom
jointed-clasped together, and that also in the sky

are dancers and musicians and a violin floating
above small rustic houses that are capped in snow
Who knows why the bride is all white, the groom

all blues? Madrid
is the green fringes
that seek out under a sky that is a premonition
where two young children whisper together
throwing shadows across the sand

is a home on the Gran Via
of pressed up cardboard pushed to a wall
that a tiled-ledge runs across
so that just above the box-home there is a shelf
with the same toy cars I owned as a child
made safe in a straight line
and a small and delicately heart shaped bottle of expensive
cheap perfume, and a few other
things tucked away in the folds of a carpet-waterproof-coverlet thrown
over the whole constructed abode

No inhabitant could hold
the constant rush
of passers by Madrid is

the flux in the musculature of the standing bear
that shakes a Madrono Tree on Sol square

is alive inside of a glass house
that was once a botanic house, and now has
plates of blue acrylic, or plastic, hangings that have

punctuation marks, question marks, parenthesis, set in
-to them as transparencies
allowing the light in
so that what is outside of the sun or stars
may communicate with what ever

is inside Madrid

is the Barco Solar El Retiro approaching
the wooden jetty where all the rowboats are
sculling oars to dock, and empty

and fill again, it is there in the sprays
of a waterfall splitting light into spectra
where trees are parched grey
bark a skin peeling in the shrinking away of
a without leaf that rises
out of the dust Madrid is

an everywhere is crowds of people carrying
balloons, waiting to ride the boats, eating
nuts they crack out of shells that are thrown
families, children, courting couples, marchers
and strollers talking, talking, or manning stalls
carrying cardigans, or coats, music sounding
out of headphones, picture takers, phoners,
gamers, pushers of boys on plastic trikes
wearing trainers, white shoes, mountain boots
dark sunglasses, hats with shades, holders
of balloons on strings, answering things,
gathering into crowds of watching and clapping

something that happens in the midst of them,
servers at stalls looking into prams, who peer
curiously through iron railings, carry coats
baring their skin, hold the exit gates open, kick
footballs in the air and run, press badges on
to blouses, stand and watch as others step on
to boats, kissing each other just the once upon
each cheek, carry bottled water, are babies
crying persistently, gratingly, putting small caps
on children's heads, raising up flags, shouting and
singing along to a music playing just for them

small birds chatter in apertures set deep in
the trunks of grey trees, or flit

as two small boys sword-fight long balloons
run and stamp their feet, or trail
the points, stirring up dust,
or climb railings just to feel the pull against them,
all weight, concentrated hard

birds sit the bare branches, flit

breathless about the dust bath Madrid is

this man in a red shirt and Raven trousers who has
a just too narrow to fit, theatrically tall hat,
who sets balls of all different sizes down overly precisely

inside the circle he makes dripping water from a bottle,
irrigating the too-hot dusty street
After falling into a hand stand, he
balances balls on the flat of his head, and whistles
a crowd to appear, that claps as he shouts
and laughs when he entreats the children sit near,
watch the show, and please do throw

the multicoloured skittles back, Madrid, Madrid

is a man always frayed at the edges

is the red dust that stains

plosive scrapping on

blackfeatheredmuscledlightbrightyellowbeaksflashswooping
rustlingcrackfluster confusions in the branches
one chasing language

one escaping delineates to ground noisily
and sudden, unlooked for, rabbit, young, ran

out the bush and was gone
to see one here, one, this year—when i had supposed them all drowned

To Ithaca

we stepped out of the streets
where commerce was busy defeating the rain
to the stillness of silk

a Kesa in a glass cage
stitched together of precious remnants
elaborately embroidered with lotus flowers

the raw silk the colour of old bone
or *gleaming on a body like the skin of a dried onion**
smooth, reflecting the sun.

a reverenced cocoon.
the uniforms of Japan's firefighters
in the days before safety

were as colourful and fragile as their young lives.
the mulberry leaves transformed in nature
from one state to another and woven together

stronger, with all ceremony
and reverence and care, were treasures.
gifts of the past made new.

the idea of a warm sun held to a skin,
the hope of continuation, of something vital enduring.

---

*italics are paraphrased part of Odysseus's description—when in disguise
—of his own undershirt—as told in answer to Penelope in order to satisfy
her that he (a traveller) had met Odysseus—her husband.

Little feats

after Lisa

She tells him that his feet are too small for him to be standing up

that he must surely fall
that gravity and good sense dictate as much
and that in refusing to obey their laws he makes himself
subject to the disgrace of dancing in public

like one of his forebears did (all for a drink)
that they run in the blood
that no good can come of it

She does not know about the hours of crossing on a wire
from building to building

or all of the windows entered blindly when the doors were shut
All the practise put in before he ventured out

wild garlic in the rain

him sitting on the sofa that bursts out in springs
and is like him, a straw man, leaking
all over the place unable to restrain any
impulses, unable to retain any
grace and the source of all the worries
a leathered wet skin split and bleeding.

About the base discarded emptied tins of beer
ten or so the measure of how he's here
in hiding, really, behind a stupid grin
every gesture extra large lets everybody in

behind his defences, though there is some thing still
unreachable, hidden deep beneath the stuffing.

A thought bought him here to tip amongst wild flowers
took away his legs and seated him as the showers
washed out leaving coal rimmed eyes and flattened hair.

An abandoned dog cries not knowing which
way to go to get back to the comfortable home that it

once knew. He remains an emptied sack
spilling the clues you'll take the time to piece back
together, making good, and bringing to an end
all this bad weather. Droplets fill the bright flower-heads
and fall as the petals tilt to
under the skies falling weight.

'They just don't build like this anymore.' he says,
battering on the arms, 'There's no craftsmanship, no days,
put into them, they're just turned out by the score. Once men . . .'

beyond crack willow

black capped gull fusses an edge
of a sort of starting silted island
that is almost shore but is divided
opposing two rivers push together
bodies interlocking planes of cool
water throwing stunted limbs
that peak and circle back on to
or out from inlets that gull struts
perhaps protects, glisten streams
emerge from the rheumy green
reflections of border trees before
a convergence when slow deep
channels gather a dark sleeking
of round stones safe translucence
from the prying hot sun. A
shiny metal beer can turns
passes by the red clay banks
by the sticky leaf'd sycamores
stringy offerings of green
clustered insect headed flowers
by the tall pointed grasses that
puncture as the crowded teeth
of daisies welcome. Here
a shush of water steps down
the weirs hesitant stalactites,
to diaphanous shallows where
midges air in black knots of
misaligned matter evasively
pirouetting over scrub reed
borders to unpeopled water,
and bird   chits   follow
this way, follow this way

its arrow head a calciferous
skull stutters of lustrous coal,
is nibbed stone, is crocked flint,
it fans the sonorous lung—
shallows till crack windfull
wings are all sudden fastened
shadow infolds, and content
edges in waters eddies and flows

Out there

in the white white white of far
sticking summer of spring silks
pussy willow downs are softly moulting
an impermanence of striking bells
roll calls black and light
days—blank pages—new leaves
each a caterpillar igloo to freefall
in patterns barely discernible
from such a distance, as though a glaze
freezes and melts simultaneously
makes a still frieze of landscape
where sheets of ice meld
refracting and reflecting structures
such as they briefly are, opaquely
visible and yet invisible
to be lost again to the wind
as low afternoon sun floats
four sheets high to the high winds
where words fly, must fly
to fade into the haze

Clean

the break of morning in my hands
was cupped, did flow
and in the falling returned without
the usual blessing to the sink below

a silver line, though that's not true
turned milky white or brown with grime
i splashed, not dabbed, as parishioners do
who dab themselves each time
they leave the house in want
of a blessing, perhaps remembering

the first break of breath
to leave its warm embrace

once it left, slavered, from a crack in the ground
to a trickle, a flow, and racing gathered
a mossy frond around
turned from fast to slow

ponderous and strong it moved the earth
to wear a way and join with others
to a vast ocean i have no conception of

was lost as sweat or piss, became
condensation, a cloud that gathers
or perhaps was a tear of dew

here it begins each day's drenching
not as cold as a mountain stream
has no trace of frog or fish
that wild in nature could be a risk
does not take the breath away

to impart the chill of cool
or the thrill of day

hard here and now

solid as a railway sleeper, hard and thick
you can drive a knife right into it,
if you're a physicist

go cut off a slither, or pull on a splinter
that has somehow lodged deep in a finger,
burrowed under skin
and gone to rest.

inviting as a new idea, lit and beckoning
lacking any sense on closer reckoning.
always just coming or having just gone
you can't pin it down, it lacks all reason,
travelling with you like a second,
third, or fourth, skin, and the rest.

an iris

soaked then left to air
its longish petals now slight as paper
curl to tapers at the edges,
and lightening yield to a white at centre
as if bleached at the join, where yellow
tipped stamens are the crown
of a faded kingdom that has known
glories, has become used
to too many unchanging
and relentlessly new suns.
                              there is
thinness without brittle fragility. it is

this days start, an endurance,
one more
              thump
of a heart that turning every
-thing over once again,
                              ignites
the sweet sap that firms petals
                              and feeds.

sleeping these are the remote stretchings
of planets escaping a sun, they furl
into water sliding under itself, and over
in waves foaming white at each swell.

within arteries the soils blood
running to charges of light calls bees
or other insect kind, feed
on the changing dew, rewrite it

as lovers might do.
                                    here is the soft
of gravel pits at the centre of a bed
of leafs spiked like pointed tongues.

A blue eye nods open—a recognition

Intent

In that tent was all I could need
and every morning a van came
delivering breakfast milk and eggs
not too early, I could lie in
recover from the night before, slowly
stretch my back into shape;
watch her condense air into fresh
shapes from the tip of nose and curl

of hair visible; consider the rucksacks
upright against the tent poles; listen
to the sounds outside this thin partition
of nylon, the grass swaying, the footsteps
of other campers cooking and swearing
as they waken stiff and unzip the day.

Blackberries and Ice cream Jazz

Waiting alongside the railway line
flowers opened on a branch, butterflies
alighting—Blue Morphos—as fine as
Gentians, finer, delicate as moths caught in long

tongues of light, tongues as long as the fat vase
of their bodies—sipping at the flowers
                                  of pullman coaches
arms outstretched
                    are stretched towards a refusal.

here there are no charms or lucky heathers
                              hemmed into rough skirts
or into the strange geometries of
                wind disturbed leaves busied up
                        against great coats.

There are ears like bent thumbs
                    waiting to be filled with the cries
of barrow boys

or hmmm hmmmm suits
              with bright red ties.

The street is red, not burgundy, but a hot powder is dust
              to the subway
                    of impudence
of blossoms pink as errant corn,

when the river is blue as cold.

Versification error

there's a random versification error in line 76
this train can't leave the platform
sleeping leaves are stacked up like bricks
crisp and yellow and perfectly formed
they obtrude onto the track
deluding the system into thinking that
a body, solid, living or dead
or in transition, has fallen like lead
and come to a stop right there in the path
of commuters and tourists and railway staff

what can we do, how will it end?
manually we must gather them and blend
a new fabric, laced, without any ribbing,
natural, organic, that holds words without ripping
and falls to the floor at the end of each line
to rot straight away in perfect real time

Ovid at the water

of the water
of the body of it lying flat
pressed down flat by the solid weight
of air above it—

pushing down and pinching it to explore
and tease itself out
into every nook and cranny
of the hard uneven rock-bed until it bears
fairly—the whole
mass spreading in obedient surface to take
any number of riders
from the ragged flotilla of small boats tethered
to one jetty or another

a surface—that if you like is a face
of being—a mirror content to erase
itself concealing its nature
to play a mere part of whatever
surrounds—like an unsure
person at a party—who knows no-one—and seeks
a hidden corner—all desire
hot balled within—watching
tremulous the goings on

at the wooden sheds where the boats are put away
while the wind unhooks leaves to break free
of a clutch of holding trees—and be
alone momentarily as they fall
to where others have gathered
in various states of decomposition

leaving almost naked the trees that claw at clouds
for concealment and cause them to change
from one animal shape to another

an old wolf rears up becoming a bear
collapses and topples over
into itself before separating out to a pack
of wolves that slackly metamorphose

while geese idle to shelter
easing from water while it is still
and has a slate grey face that is impenetrable

every frame is too fragile to contain
all of this—yet is taken in
clean by the water until waves appear
cropping the surface and jostling

riders short leashed to the jetties
become horses sensing danger
wet nosed mustering
splayed great-hoov'd feet

the thunder of manes and tails
a knowing bristle in the air

attic-headed

Aware of the sleeping he slept
where the wide eaves were live wires and the brick was raw
Two panes admitted light that waned and was extinguished
somewhere halfway across a rock board floor

The only furniture a pine bed a pine dresser and hid
behind the door was a high backed chair
her father had made that could no longer be trusted
being always in need of urgent repair

Where light holds is a plain living
Beyond a blackness reigns
he would walk into and disappear
but at this height he is weightless

unpacking dreams that send out runners
to shoot and root in-
toxicatingly fruiting mellow offspring blooms
in hothouse rooms Stairwell lovers meet

Too late! Too late! The feet upon the stair
will break apart the furniture
berating those who only sleep
The sea an inky-blue wash speaks

to impatient rocks in whispers
Far off yachts move slowly in the absence
of serious wind Sleepers lie
on a concrete wall dividing

land and sea as if they are stone
staring upwards through closed eyelids

Stertorous man Heron flys
gathering furrows to make an island

between the lobes and consume whatever
cares should rise like hot loaves

Heron

6th

Saw a heron eat a little slither
of the silver river

9th

Maybe the heron that I thought a man
                    is, was a woman
                    —somehow melancholy
when cloud obscures the sun it is
curiously a shroud raised upright on the water
and when the light is full on
the unlikely brand of itself appears
root legs cutting against all baffled direction
planted bloodless feet toes holding
to the silt river bed. Is it
a woman weeping?

I see her sometimes standing—alone
a shabby kind of a creature—not
wandering—not old—not young

thorny, so that to reach out and touch her
she will snap—beyond speech—
her sharp beak at the Gulls
concerted diving
in order to drive her from this thin spit
she has claimed hers, more an island really
                    —not even a dot on a map
                    as the earth is lost on a star map

a raised up held fast loose rest of shingles
concentrated, fixed to a place by the roots
of some low scrub
so that when the river is low even the cows come
down here to nibble at some nameless herb

        they can find no-where else.

Descartes running away . . .

it is possible the Crows think me
a large wasteful being
profligate even
twisting off and throwing them
pieces of pastry

swollen as it is the River does not waste
it tests to find a use for each thing
refusing no thing
to fill the place
it was all those years diverted from

remember when it just stopped
short of entering
the house we lived in
peaceably
no lock could have withstood it

this day the lights go on
in the centre of town

yet what holds
are three Crows

who flit branch to branch nearer
to where what is thrown drops
on the thin margin remains
between the form and the
waters edge

cold? it is not!
dark? it is

though not so dark that they are not darkest

the rehearsed fates
appearing at once
like clumsy gatecrashers
at a somewhat worn party

whose utterances utterly alien might be
pleads in another language
that these ears untrained
can not connect with hunger or with a longing

for company of any sort whatsoever

any ear
and they spill out thoughts that gather into cloud
filling the sky

there is much earth in the River

wind-stripped branches and logs float by
(anything would) as it cuts into banks that held it back so long
diligently undermining them

when rains come again there will be no holding
no reins

and servitude will be history
as it takes back the stubble land

to rub the dry stones smooth with wet

the unreachable trembling as its stretched arms feel out blindly
across flatlands uniting
the claimed tributes of each stream

finding out old roads and following

it is not so cold that Crows are thin
but then are they ever thin that will feast on whatever

perished before them?
they are
formless lumps at distance stumbling
over furrows making strange cries
closing in
close to close enough to see

unflinching unreadable eyes
black depths holding things caught weightless

impossible to judge

rather than fine black silks fine black feathers

and I the suspect in the dock am
guilty of course   how could I not be

reflections

they are a line walking across a line
of crude planks battened together to make
a path of sorts that is some-places dry
yet seeps. Everywhere seeps
water from under the low bridge—seeps
about what remains of trees that rise
end on end from the churned up mud each side.
The denuded branches broken fingers
standing for a mighty forest.

Each man wears long boots, and a heavy belt
secures a canvas bag close to the skirt
of a military jacket. Eyes
the terrain from under a steel helmet.

The air is grey—no other colour—grey,
as if only smoke or mist or what remains
of a smoke or of a mist lives here.

It could be that these five men are the last
—perhaps stragglers somehow become lost,
or perhaps they walk slowly to an uncertain rest
after setting down this damp makeshift

causeway. glisten thin sheets of still
water mirror the broken lines

of trees and the pale skies,
and though some of the trees are reflected,
petrified, the men appear all alone

begin

when you can reach up and take a strand of light
straight as a laser beam and splitting it weave
a basket capacious enough to carry this day
and the next, and after, i will accompany you
down to the swollen river where the dark water is
held on course by mud flats and green scrub banks
and we will be young again and these three days
all we will need, or can imagine, and stretching
a measure of ourselves in the lush grass while more
than our bodies weight passes each moment
time will still as it used to do into an eternity, until . . .
well, until . . . . .

Compounds and Fire

Mayflies

A bridge of orange clay
on a steel tubular frame
is where mayflies flit.

Delicate sets of wings
beat asynchronously
about each planet's

long tapering body
—a fidget of the air,
eccentric and giddy,

moving above the water
it hatched out of.
Polished steel and dull clay

worked into position
joins beginning to end,
has a purpose in a

way the slow running
river, and dithering
Mayflies do not.

The river eats
into the rough banks
that peel away

on either side,
gorges itself each high tide.
Mayflies sip at

dead shivers of air,
devils hanging there
learning its language

Wasp

A faint buzzing at the ears
uncomfortably nears

It is a mystery how they keep on coming in

I would throw them out
all of them
astonished pieces
of a larger thing

What a society is
is something that coheres

These yellow and black bands are a mark, perhaps
of self sacrificing

The feared sting being something
that must be taken on

drawn out of them
from the rapture of the bodies spindle

its drill precision
urgently braced within the legs rigging

There is no knowing the thing apart
unmassed, outside of its cauldron

One, undone,
has broken the muttered vow of its own

making to surrender all thought of motion
and be paper-dry and brittle

A sculpture on the ledge
its worrying head black metal

Productions

In the finished goods warehouse Danny ruled
with operatic efficiency

brogue irish arias connecting the stacks
of pallets in the rows

the italian in his soul steaming out
songs and whistles

'sounds and sweet airs'

At the bleach spillers the caustic liquid
made concrete slippery

for the women behind the masks and gloves
who anonymously fed

the lines shouting to be heard
in all of the heat

The red floor still divided into sunken squares
was where liquid soap used be poured

allowed to dry before being
hoked up into flakes

when the canal brought whale oil and steam
took what was made away

No-one knew what the piano was doing
it had no business being carefully set

directly under where the forklift broke through
a mezzanine rail, and fell

Voyage

I sleep above spreading trees
where birds with wild plumage roost
and in a glade a deer grazes
while another passing nibs
discrete grasses amongst the flowers
as birds sing having nothing
to do all the ease full days
but see the leaves change, and fall
away to make a bed so rich
seeds growing toes dig and twist
to heads that climb, and arms that spread
making the trees that made the bed
of non-existence I sleep above

until the trees go the way of love

Age

whenever he lost the use of his arms
she would dress him in the morning
with fistfuls of sky brushed free of cloud

spoon him joy that chuckled out of the ground
constantly where streams of clear bubbled
refreshing the dry earth set with limber trees
across the valley floor and up bared scree to the toes
of the mountains, and the austere realm of rocks
and drier things, and he would become as spiky
as a cactus standing alone whipped by sands
that are dervishes unrelenting wild and dancing
the dance each day brings in moaning lament
of want of aught to do but tend the fire

she sets to hold him like a wire

how to survive

all across the plot
grew gourds, alien shapes,
lantern colours, they draped
their heavy selves across the branches
of fruit trees, hanging

until ripe. cutting

them down finds
a thick skin, a rind
to break any knife's thin blade.

baking the strange pots in a hot oven
only makes them harder. We tried

drilling, and found no way

in to the flesh. Years on

found them festooning the trees in Kowloon

tissue papers with a heart of flame.

Wild Garlic Reprise

up early always up early he wears
a washed clean white newly creased
and a tie he always does
sees the flowers planted out in rows
in the four foot square
bite of land out back
as the kettle boils he makes a snack for later on
tomato and a slice of ham no pickle left today
wishes it done and on his way
mutes the TV dumb
whatever is on seems insane
the same old lies told again and whatever
cord pulled him in is broken now
he's floating in an unknown sea
of misery pulled tight around
sinking in a shifting ground he
hums a tune to hear a sound and it calls to him
the women who knew who wanted in
to where he waits abiding time

except for when he sleeps he's fine

In the corners where sleep gathers

unknown

A man that I had known as a boy
shot the two young horses each with one bullet
to the centre of their foreheads, a terrible third eye

the beautiful white horse sought me out for comfort
nuzzled my hand so that i must rest it flat
on the blood wet nose as the ugly wound wept

the wound was a flower whose petals peeled back
revealed a hole at its centre where the stamens and stigma
should be as the life slowly drained away

i wanted to leave, to run away, but the horse was so beautiful
its need so acute that i was rooted there
afraid that it might turn on me, and bite

it died gently, and the black horse that had curried in to its side.
i wept at the lose of such beauty and grace
as if some part of my self had died.

Bog man

Black, hard and heavy,
dried solid with all the acid liquid compacted out, he stands
strange, though in keeping with this room
and its warm walls of blood
that viewed through closed eyelids on a bright summers day,
make a maternal space that calmly includes,
and connects this small god
to her. An early icon
standing guard with a crook on his right arm,
he faces out from the mantle. No traces
remain of the slit trench, his birthing scar.
No sign of where he was taken.
Man and man before dug the peat there
and dried it for fire, taking cheap heat from the
bog of their land, and he was fashioned of it,
sculpted or moulded somehow to form this jet
Norseman who watches through blank eyes,
and longs to return to the place he was farmed.
Being a native of that land. Others
of his race given a half chance of learning left
the harsh life with its rule of seasons
while she was formed and rough schooled
in its foreign tongue.
                    One day they broke
away uprooting the made dark man.

Utopia

A young woman passing me had Utopia,
attractive as it happens,
inscribed upon her top, on the right
just above her breast, where she might
indicate her heart to be

because she works there, so she said
and I have absolutely no reason to disbelieve her,
Utopia being a hair dressing salon.
Her hands were shiny, dry, and worn

Smile

starting is a risky business
you never know just where a line might take you

whether a voice you hear might join you
carry on the conversation

at least a dialogue of sorts
with that girl that smiled at you that you've seen

many times in the bar
and think you saw pushing

a baby in a pram recently
with an older man, much older than her, anyway

so if her smile won't clear from your mind what will you do
to make sense

and what is the point of this exercise
excepting that it is in itself an exercise

and that the more that you write the easier it will get
although obviously this hasn't happened yet

for the more you try the more mind drifts
from any discernible object it could have

and appears without purpose
and even the fleet beauty of that smile that encompassed

eyes, nose and mouth, begins to fade
amongst the dense and growing undergrowth

which all goes to show that the very premise
of practise is incorrect,

and that you should have stopped,
perhaps been forced to, long ago.

Woken

US US US US US US US US
wakes me.

I picture a crow, or some dishevelled bird
alone on the roof
a fledgling perhaps
sobbing for company
that not having taken to wing
is frightened of falling
and abandoned
must consider that step into nothing
but air

the slight curved feather

the slight curved feather saved from the fallen
tucked in between the print of a painting of an unknown
woman, against the wall, is softly held and pliable
all of its ribs shiver as it peeps from her gathered up hair
the wells of her eyes look out the infinite, and suffer
smoulderingly blurry as twin black holes above a
blunted nose that divides an oily yellow-fleshed moon
down to the chasm of a mouth that also seems prim
is also waiting somehow, the parted lips are bruised
on rather than brushed in to the thick mastic paint
layered on, and worked on, again, and this feather is
much too frivolous to be here where there are no whispered
accusations hiding in the corners, and her aching breasts
are covered and shielded from all of the naked silences

low moon

how strange to see a low full moon
hanging there

a dustbin lid, a round luminescent door
lighting in the air

an off milk flower with invisible stem
a plate caught in suspension

just within reach of fingertips
i could run my fingers around a rim of craters

fill in blue algae oceans
with a marker pen
fix brown green colours
to make what? not an earth

made smooth by such distance
cold without a stitch of life
but bare rock, no rivers or trees
and bone bone dry

no—there's nothing but dust
no soil that warm loam clot
no worms or mould or leaf
its stone, a wind worn crust

no thing disturbs its surface
except perhaps the scour wind circling
muttering, howling
rusting rock

unheard telling out the days
how strange it looks.

Oedipus

sun was a straight white line coming
in at the cracked lip of the front door
silently, even the birds were standing
wait on dog slates toeing an edge of gutters
and rooftops, and looking out from here
for what might break fast of night, or
shake free and warm a cold blood
uncertainly brooding in the air, would
sip out things before leaving the lair
to clothe itself in soiled leaves and pass
black hole eyes that draw down energies
lashing out and making violent seas,
perforating all of those honeycomb
doors locked up and named a home

an other wave

betting a brother at a wedding once separated people
into wavers and non wavers
the wavers returned a wave happy and smiling
the non wavers embarrassed would sit ignoring
us waving at them, disconcerted

when a wave returned we would be delighted
as though an important fact of contact had been made
even without speaking, without words
the action and mode of waving would indicate a character
aware that this silly gesture across space
full of loud small talk and music
raced quickly to the heart of the thing
the ridiculous hope in our being here all crowded together
alone and waving

excerpt 1 from Blackness library
—and other inconsequential things

inside there are
blooms in the back parlour
spun of tender vibrations

day was wet clay and noise until men
abandoned the cement mixers, dumper trucks,
and diggers to us who played on them
after hours, when each was a bright splinter
blossoming at the tree-lined street corner
on a plot of waste land where fires lit
night flowers against a darkening sky. Spitting
stars of sputters eased us of the terrors
waiting, always waiting, out there

excerpt 2 from Blackness library
—and other inconsequential things

down our street
the butcher has two rabbits.
he cuts off the hands and feet.
cuts off each head.
pulls away the blood-furred skin.
peeling them open
slicing into the peritoneum
the miniature organs set within.
such intricate viscera. the mechanisms.
the hearts no bigger than thumbs.
tips wagging

days balanced on the branches of trees
or on high stone walls as they worked
themselves to where stale bread thrown
on window ledges sat with the dried
disengaged shells of insects. or
they tramped aimlessly on up the moor
fitfully tugging at tongues that wagged
and blistered hands that shook pulling
to those places that looked out girls
until the earth turned on its axis

falling to a glass
that twitches
like a compass needle's
under-skin . . .

excerpt 3 from Blackness library
—and other inconsequential things

it took everyone a while
to find their place within the sprawl
of the milk products whey and cheese factory
to learn the hygiene routines, the colour
coded overshoes, hair-nets, suits and gloves
worn all times in the different production areas
to ensure that absolutely no touch of the human,
no hair or skin with who knows what
could get in and contaminate the goods

we all looked the same from the small distance
of the safety lenses
working through the off milk smell, and smelled
the same, of off milk and all of the disinfectants
used in cleaning the stainless steel

as hydrochlorics and caustics steamed our skin,
in a heat that in summer would quickly bring
a sweat rash to itching as we moved things
hot in disposable suits, disposable beings
computer monitored raising the clots
that formed, and crushing them into blocks

Virgin

Hair severely
centre-parted, plaited, reads
'a winter birth', hides away
holding it before her face.
Everybody else chatters in
the quiet coach. 'Better
get my shit together'
the singer sings in my ear.
This is coach A.

Trees pass, telegraph
poles, grasses, moss,
cloudy and cloudless skies. We sit
confident in the plastic
tube, removed. This is
coach A. A teacher

from Lancaster University reads
an essay entitled 'Dark and cold
and rugged is the North: Elizabeth
Gaskell, Charlotte Bronte, and
Northern Gothic', adding pencil
notes in a soft grey hand that
disappears amongst the bold
black laser print. This is

coach A Quiet zone. A hot
spot. Fast reliable internet.
There is Springwater in clear plastic.
Buildings pass. Windows blankly
stare. Rough brambled embankments.
A steeple. Brick walls. We

breath in plastic, go. Lads
loiter on a platform edge
underneath a low steel bridge.
We pour off, on, a liquid
membrane of us ruptures, and then
seals up again. Singer sings
'This isn't working my little grass
-hopper'. Platform 4.
Mobile masts, houses, trees. Notice
the essay is set-out double-spaced.
Himalayan Balsams proliferate.
Pages turn. Announcer announces
'All tickets and passes please',
stirring us up into a wave

of reaching and opening. The fire
extinguisher is located in the
vestibule. 'Rubbish please'. 'Stow
all luggage'. Singer says 'Walk away
now, your gonna start a war'.
Gun metal grey industrial
units, pipework, low rises, high
rises, semi detached, terraces.
Another low bridge. Himalayan
Balsams, White Willow. A canal
is a breaking line crossing a field
of Fressians. Black sacks, hay
stubble, disused factories
with roofs caved in, opened
to the elements. Useless
as a shelter. This

is coach A. Smoking is
not permitted on this train. For
coach letter see electronic displays.
Corn yellow stubble. Please ensure
that you take everything
with you. A rugby field. Please use
the racks for large and hard bags only.
Chemical factories, pylons, trees,
a drop to water, trees, factories.
Leaves scrape against the window. Speech
is a foreign language of Mobile
rings, cuts off. The woman scratches
then smooths her hair down. Adjusts
her bra strap. Resumes reading.

Wolves

beyond the comically wind ruffled
crow at his station
on the uppermost stanchion
of the steel bridge, I saw
two black wolves
sleek and feral

crow rose to fly
as a man was crossing
who turned right along the river
as they were reduced to dogs

two ducks quarrelled
then one flew a small distance
to settle pecking at its wing
amongst the scrub of the waters edge

until stopped by Max's scampering
play friendly snub-nosed mongrelling
'Only four months old' laughed man
'Everything's new to him' smiled woman
leading him back on to the path

the rippled surface of cold black water is a hard thing
constantly changing in its flows
is forbidding
and I'm drawn towards it

down in the old deeps wolf packs run
shoulder to shoulder
and I am a follower
all the way down to the white tresses of the rapids

Kites

We didn't see until we followed the line
The small brightly coloured kite
Up there, anchored tight to him
'Why would you want to do that?'
You said dismissively, watching
As he guided it into a swoop
Let it take the wind, and falling
Exerted skill so it would soar again

Riding the squalls, and be of them.
Alone, solitary in that field
Buffeted as the same wind took his hair
Tugged his clothing

While the kite, tilted to the wind, sailed high
Alive in its changing breath

'Grandfather would make kites with newspaper, sticks, and string
and when I was young we would paint them
Take them out
And see if they could fly

See if the winds would take them
Like an offering'

in Firenze art

is a white stone vein running
down David's arm, that unable to flex
calls along the stretching cord of itself
to the softnesses of stolen corpses hid
with such a confident grace, they beat
in a chest that is a stone wall of muscle

whose tide has set, and flesh cells
—cells of marble that these others
—four prisoners, unfinished as yet, struggle
to be free of, struggle to wake.

There is a temporary exhibit on
perfection in form
with Venus tied and bound,
headless, his arms out

-stretched as if on a cross
formed of delicious flowers, made architectural.
And next to this David there is Thomas
crouched up inside of a concrete cylinder
his black muscular shoulders hunched

wrestle out, as if oppressed
by the promise of the weight of all of this

after the fall

frightened as i was of the damage
of an unintentionally firm squeeze
these fingers spread to fold down your wings
safe over a soft feathery body
so warm and pliably boned that there must be
a heart lighter than air that pulled
upwards against gravity to the whites
of the openable sky where you would fly

you had no fear i could see
in giving yourself over to me
as i lifted you out through the solid black iron
aperture that had held you in
after such a soundless alarm
it seemed you tuned an ear to every breath

On the days

after and dedicated to Nazim Hikmet

sea entered in
and the knots that stained the 'old varnish' of walnut
called on the heavy sound of ripe walnuts dropping onto a tin roof
and the rich spreading blackness of the trees soaking up the sun
its waves, the branches infinite oceans
on these days I am
sea and cloud and the sap flowing
am the life that warms cold iron,
                              or melts a block of ice in a pan
on these days there can be no separation
there are no boundaries
and skin has no meaning except that touch happens
and feeling
and pleasure can
on these days I think of the day of my birth leading
up to all of this
movement and stillness in light
ribs lifting and falling in breath
and everything is right suddenly
even death - if I could choose
when to die it would be on a day like this
with the sun warm, not so high, not so strong that the eye needs
to be averted, with soft winds sounding the branches,
when there is nothing important to be done except being
witness to all of this
the tarnished foil of a fishes eye
the push-me pull-you waves
a seagull chick with a ripped and bleeding wing attempting
—futilely to fly
even the lies of a media that crush
compressing what is best of us
to flowers and leaves in a book, but
this day the leaves are all nimble
as the scales of small fish that dart light
as raindrops squeezing through hairline cracks that serve
to make musical notes ripple in a still pool

Time

saps the serious curiosity of cows lined against the fence
night barn smells about their swinging nuzzle dewed chins
and damped eyes old as varnished wood maternally
look, a grandfathers eyes, a brothers, load
bearing eyes that seem to be open and closed, calm
and uneasy. The kind of eyes that you
might imagine law makers to possess, old

testament eyes, perhaps. They take
warm sun like a medicine holding close together
at the rail, throwing shadows undressed vague forms,
loose echoes, or black flowers, on the turned ground,
chewing the last of the hay. Their mahogany
eyes dark holes that reach for light
in fields so big that they forget.

cancer plate

it broke, the plate of his cancer
being much more of a plate than a bowl
flat and low rimmed

the vein of it seemed to circle off centre
as though the core was out of the picture
but the slender stem remains
rim cracked, and the use has flown

SF soft dissolve

in order to go
I sprayed something from an aerosol onto her flat
warm stomach that
loosened the molecular,
then clambered inside what had been her,
head and shoulders first
so that she was now circling about what was
me that had become loosened too
that had joined with her to a universe
of floating particles and absolutely empty space
where thought was dissociated from
everything that could, and might, be formed,
was so cold that it simply could not join
itself to any other being

socks

At the base of two flights
of stairs I found
I had her socks,
smaller pink socks
she must have misplaced
inside my shoes,
the muddled night before, and they
had somehow become tangled,
had intertwined,
each of hers with one of mine.

I climbed back up to find her newly
purchased boots, and loosed her
socks before moving on,
each one swallowed in a boots undone throat.

Senses

Every thread lost itself and was re-found.
I recognised the sound
of the whole being greater than the parts;
of accord that stops and discord that starts;
loud as a mill floor in full sweats, heard
the turning mechanisms of a wind up bird.
Grinding gears forcing complainant wings
to open up and then close down again;
metal head turning as if to stare;
eyes dead pools of empty cares;
such heavy feet pounding on the ground
berating in a dance of round, and round,
to the awful croak of a plastic beak.
Sleeping i listen hoping soon to wake.

Havana Scene

Open-backed wagon offloads
varieties of Marrows and Carrots below
the balcony of the building opposite
with a corrugated roof.
Old man sits on a bicycle and talks
to younger and darker man. Dog licks
at a puddle. People gather and wait
at the side of the road for the bus to come.
People lean out on their balconies chatting.
People repair cars, smoke, or don't smoke,
put out washing, or carry chairs
that have been repaired. People walk,
drive, or pedal passed. Skin is hot.
Sky is so intense a blue that white
cloud is an exclamation of unusual intent.
Elderly lady wears an orange top
and a brown skirt carries a plastic bucket
across the street to where man has a satchel
waits by the corner. Woman comes
out onto the balcony opposite to comb
the wet from her hair. Child looks
out at the blue waggon leaving with carrots
that remain of its load. Boy and girl
chat through iron railings. She is pointing
out something on the next balcony where
two young women are leaning and chatting.
Talking with their hands and lips and shoulders.
Their brightly coloured towels fluttering

Circa, sus partes en mi paisaje

Arturo Cuenca

A lighter than some
skinned woman
sits on a bench
in what must be
a park, her right
arm on the back
resting, her left
hand on the closed
book in her lap.

Much of the park
grounds are white
or close-off white
and her face, her nose
and mouth blend out
into the off-white
so that the features
of her nose and mouth
are indistinguishable.

          Her blouse
is almost mostly white, though
above her white breast
is a blue and red
pattern—like a flower
but not a flower
and her skirt is a blue
denim colour, dark
in the foreground.

          Some light
and dark green grass,

and another bench figures
in the top right corner
as well as what might
be a streetlamp. The

thing that draws the eye
to all this is the expression
of languid determination
                    in the eye
of the young woman
as she gazes
though we only see one
                    eye
we imagine the other
and her right hand
seems to flow
from the back of the bench, and
become solid fingers
from a molten—or no
not molten—from a
gaseous insubstantiality—these
two things suggesting
both a dream state, and
the instability of the matter
of the everyday

The Vegetable Garden, New York

Cholov Yisreal Pas Yisreal Shomer Shabbat

Voice of a reasonable female repeats
the phrase 'new seamless order'
'new seamless order'
as the man crouched behind the food counter
—a bearded man wearing that small round cloth cap that I forgot
the name of just then—that is hairpinned on, and that now I refuse
to look-up in the Dictionary;
the very pleasant and courteous man who swears again,
I think—in Yiddish,
unable to contain himself or hold the wealth of
words from tumbling out under his breath
as he pulls at the tangle
of wires on the shelf at the far back of the till
where a laptop is set up along side his paperwork.

The screen lights the message
'seamless web' and the endlessly becoming
tangle is more and more
convoluted, and complex, and a telephone calls out
advising him of something, and of all this reminds
of a scene in the film *Brazil* where the character played by Robert De Niro
—a plumber or some kind of maintenance guy—
opens a grill found on the wall of an artificial room—a cabin—
that tubes
and wires spill from
filling everywhere—like intestines would do,
or might if somebody sliced open an abdomen. He'd pushed
them back in—and clamboured inside of the cavity himself,
battling with the fluid workings until some kind of order,
though none could be seen, was restored.
And then screwed
the grill onto the wall again to hold them

in place there, writhing and hissing, somehow become obscene,
and without beauty.
Looking about
there are tiles missing on the walls, the floor
is scuffed and needs repair.
The tables and chairs are really too shaky
on their pins for writing
post cards. There is
a Soup &
Sandwich &
Can of Soda
All for $8.

A customer asks for bagels. Two of everything and four
plain. She pays at the till and
as she leaves she kisses the fingers
of her free hand,
and then touches them to the words
'Cholov Yisreal' on the glass of the door.

All the orders are made up behind the wide counter
to be taken by African-American men
who come and go. One of these men
articulates a warm concern of his over money
to the bearded man who hastily counts
some notes out, and passes them over
to the man who carefully counts them too
before he folds them away and picks up the next order
for immediate delivery, and goes.

And the bodiless voice intones
'new seamless order', over and over

from a notebook purchased at
the Kafka Museum, Prague

a beginning walking old town. A has a meal of chickpeas
with spinach and cheese, K has
 pasta with a cheese sauce. fire
jugglers at dusk on the old town square
sell flaming torches to the large crowd
drifted to them.
one of the jugglers trousers have come loose and she struggles
to hold them up, and juggle.

i am more full of corners than this place is.

hotel room is large, ceiling beamed, K wishes
we had left the beams set to stand out free in our attic, like this.

the church from our window has a damaged roof and misses
many tiles. we explore

to golden lane
below the castle walls, just a row of small
houses painted brightly
that sell something, guide book tells me
formed of the waste fell away
as gold as urine

Rene Trossman sings
bending the strings of his guitar to blue shapes
that form the small cellar
and slide over to tap feet and nod heads at the bar.

at the cubist House of the Black Madonna
the entrance fee is halved after four
and in the jazz café, advertised as free, we pay

seeing Blue Fussion, and hear Weather Report and Wayne Shorter

a Jazz Boat passes on its circular

where some green conkers on thin stems are
in amongst the last of the leaves
where barely coated woman with a beagle passes
a well wrapped man with two squash faced

pug type dogs. All boats
turn before the weir
beyond The Charles, as if cogs
of a tourism mechanism. Over the river
is the Rudofinium where the 'well heeled' shelter
from the shower waiting to see 'Orpheus'
and we wait with them

seeing from within
the twinned streetlights, and less
a house than a castle, all outsiders,

strangers here, a voice says
as a Japanese lady with exotic leaf prints at each knitted jumper elbow
passes

an overweight bearded cyclist with a canvas shoulder bag
stopped to adjust his bike.

a slight breeze moves the sycamore leaves
and a part-pulled-glass of beer left to settle before

the top-up.

the river is shimmering mirror, an abstract thing, inaccurate
pulling colour from all about

to reconstruct.
there is a lot of reconstruction going on.
electric trams pass with a whirr
no clang
a young mum with two small dogs of indeterminate type on a line
joins four white swans to cross the broad wash of the water in time
to make Andante barge on the other side
and the red blue and white
flag flicks at its rear
as it continuously puffs smoke to the air
from a chimney topside. swan rears
flapping, ducks quack,

and on the Charles Bridge dark figures dart
from statue to statue

there is delicate white cloud amongst the blue
and the ground leaves are yellowed rust
and these two are too old to be let on the see-saw
fashioned simply from a log, and at the 'ethno'

are hot wines with a lemon, or orange, slice
a potato and mushroom soup that contains chicken
that smells all day on my skin
while in the Cathedral a saint has his tongue cut out

and when we see a red squirrel i almost shout—foraging

January

There's a black T-shirt
a flag left negligently
a trepidation
draped across the old iron
cannon, that trembles standing
guard on the picaresque lawn
in front of the citadel,
it's diary white
bold sedimentary letters state
'there's only one fat guy around here'.

There's a dab of melt falls from a slush bold gutter.
And I never considered before,
but who let such words out
to a place so populous with small birds
thrumming together,
gathered in a fragile assembly
of un-assembling in a darkness
that sets fire cinnamon eyes to burn
somewhere dank,
drugged up and drunk.
As dreamy as a Hodgepig
the old grunting man with a nodding scabrous head
and the counting aloud lady who sits beside him
shouting
One two three four five.
One two three four five.
One two—
pass time
preserved in a stasis of warmed soup and milky tea.

Well, we must all Away!

A swift taxi ride departure. Away
to where a heart that has only one billion beats gives up this small girl
at the last
to its own isolated beach
where smooth round pebbles are
anthracite memories she will rub between forefinger
and thumb, and throw
turning all of the waves away
that return again, ecstatically.

Endlessly.
While the blowing sea of her hair binds
an irrational wind that only Iron braids
point to as they split the sun to streaks
that race bleaching the amber her face
shrinks to a swaddling white. Look in
again, hard inside of the scuttling eyes
are bees that hide under the lids
that became estranged from the hive
or out of its reach through chasing
after the grains of each colour of that late summer.

And it occurs
dying is easy.
So very easy that there is no—

Elements still in a cooling pales, diminishes
a skin of butter to the faintest blue
under nails where the ice whistled in,
digs.

Once she was as full as any woman

and the world she thought was
dissolved in numbers
counted down from one infinity to another
each whole being changed, every level
nothing but beings just as improbable
as she who was becoming imperceptibly

smaller and looser each
day to be where the hardnesses
of the corner boys fall away

Rings off her fingers
dentures lose their fit. And
a neighbour rises, stands,
the very one that gave
the big fat gloves that kept her hands so warm.

Retiro again

Trumpeter sax bass drum
—one long tune
'The Saints' becoming 'Chatanooga Choo Choo'
besides the boating lake, and the stone Lions are whisperin'
'pardon me boy
is that the train that killed my granny? We found her bath chair,
but she wasn't there.'

But they are cold Lions. Imperial Lions. And within
the Palacio is a body laid out in state
underneath a cream plastic sheet
veined with those grey
-green earthed
veins that look like those in marble.

One World joins another
through a series of linked steps. And the loose
sheet above a mattress is a star map
of Cassiopeia and Perseus set
within a fringe of wooden clothes pegs
a gypsy might hawk down blind streets. Light,
unable to settle on the shimmering
figure of Msia Godebska on the wall
in the Thyssen, sets sail in her full
evening gown and furs that melt into a chaise-
longue that is almost, but not quite—
is it? solid, and could disappear at
any moment. Unlike
this man, whose being is slabs of colour.
Stabs of colour. Who
could not be anywhere other
than here on the terrace where the trees reach outwards and upwards

straining to hear
those conversations Olives must study? Listen
the women with orange blossom
in their hair are sharing secrets.

'The catering staff are battle droids.
And Steely Dan's never gonna do it without the fez on.'

The stretch beyond Puerta de Toleda is changed.
By the river are walkways. Trees planted.
Cyclists ride between cafés. And water . . .
sweet water flows over
what was a dry bed.
And here there are haunches

of ham (*jambon*) that hang by the door.
Platos Combinados Nison 1,
Nison 2, Nison 3, Nison 4.
Tarta de Santiago Auténtica. Para llevar.
Paper napkins litter the floor
beside the bar he sweeps. People sit *Café con leche,*
or *Té.* There is
a postcard from Segovia fills itself. Simultaneously
here and elsewhere.
There is a *Salón Comedor.* To eat
toasted croissants with jam.
On Palm
Sunday people carry Rosemary
tied up into bunches
that children chase. Or wave as if—

A delivery of *Arroz SOS,* and *Bière* arrives.

He pays
with money from behind the bar where food and money pass all day.
And where the business of dishes—
Clinking, cleaning, stacking.
The endless readying of things—

At Calle Heurtas Nozz
in the Café Jazz Populart David Gwynn
and 'Saturn Alley' carry in the blues from the US of A, and everything
is consumption.
We listen
leaning crazily against next months listing
of artists who will be spirited in.

Burnt out of a screen.

And Sol square—
where protests were—
is no-more
re-branded 'vodafone sol'. The metro's
skies are sold to Timberland'

Yet amidst the premature triumphalism of it, the trees
are people with wild hair, with arms raised.

Triptych

I   The lost box of eyes

a sensed eluding
of where she had been looking after
all of the ones that had come to her door
the young boys and the older men

diminished as she told how nervous she had been
looking after the resting
eyes that they had entrusted her with
that she would carefully place

one from each head inside a special box
though this had sometime disappeared
so that when given a man's eye to rest
she placed it carefully inside of her wet

mouth, and commenced looking about her
to find the lost box of eyes, and thought
her mouth now being full of bright
visions that they would never see right again

II   Heat

Woman who collects leaves collected sticks
they might have been roots
for they were dampened with earth
on the day that the pyre was lit
that coloured the sky to a blush
she carried the sticks to her home
as the flames reduced to a glower
placing them into a polished steel bucket
that resembled a warrior's helmet
mounted on a heavy black platter of a base
when the sticks had dried in the grate
she would break them and stack them in it
as a kindling she hoped would hold a flame
until the coals would take and warm her hearth

III   the sawdust, the ring

old in the head woman sits watching
sees the old man walk on the high wire
knows that she will see him again later
flying past her on a trapeze
eating the air
the many colours of his costume sparkling
or she will see him shuffling
toe up to toe to the very edge of an awful ravine
he will then lean into until upended
his head passes by his feet

inhaling deeply she may regret
the two of them have never met
yet he is so small he might easily fit
inside her apron pocket
where she keeps the pressed leaves
and the smooth stones that are lucky
for her
he could rest in there wittering at her waist

No dreams

in the glorious black no dreams disturbed, no images,
no thoughts, no thing, and it was beautiful
that no where, there was no weight, no form, flying was impossible
because there was no structure to fly, and the darkness
was not empty but felt full, overflowing with itself,
with the absence of everything, with nothing, and it was
neither hot nor cold, it had no feeling, or even any sense
of feeling, and no perception that it existed, or ever had,
or ever would exist, yet it some how was there,
tangible, a nothing, no light, no air
and it was glorious.